A TREASURY FOR MOTHERS

A
TREASURY
FOR
MOTHERS

compiled by Christina Koning

Michael O'Mara Books Limited

First published in Great Britain in 1998 by
Michael O'Mara Books Limited
9 Lion Yard
Tremadoc Road
London SW4 7NQ

A CIP catalogue record for this book is available from
the British Library

ISBN 1-85479-333-0

1 3 5 7 9 10 8 6 4 2

Designed by Mick Keates
Formatted by Concise Artisans
Printed and bound in Singapore by Tien Wah Press

Cover design: Slatter-Anderson
Cover image: Mary Evans Picture Library

ACKNOWLEDGEMENTS

The publishers would like to thank the following for granting permission to reproduce copyright material:
Faber & Faber for 'To My Mother' by George Barker (p.6); Weidenfeld & Nicolson for *The Millstone* by Margaret
Drabble (p.39); Little, Brown & Co for *The Women's Room* by Marilyn French (p.13), *A Boy in the Family* by
Sophie Parkin (p.42), *At Mrs Lippincote's* by Elizabeth Taylor (p.16) and for *This Crying Thing* by Kate Saunders (p.29);
Random House for *Significant Moments in the Life of My Mother* by Margaret Atwood (p.30),
The Great Umbilical by Rachel Billington (p.33) and for 'My Mother's Sister' by C. Day-Lewis (p.24); Sheil Land
Associates for *Our Kate* by Catherine Cookson (MacDonald & Co.), © Catherine Cookson 1969 (p.21);
The Wyhe Agency for *Time and Tide* by Edna O'Brien (p.27); The Society of Authors as the Literary
Representative of the Estate of John Masefield for 'C. L. M.' by John Masefield (p.6); A. P. Watt Ltd.
for 'Among School Children' by W. B. Yeates (p.20).

Whilst every effort has been made to trace the owners of copyright material, in a few cases this has proved
to be problematic and so we take this opportunity to offer our apologies to any copyright holders whose
rights we may have unwittingly infringed.

Thou art thy mother's glass, and she in thee
calls back the lovely April of her prime...
WILLIAM SHAKESPEARE - SONNETS

In the dark womb where I began
My mother's life made me a man.
Through all the months of human birth
Her beauty fed my common earth.
I cannot see, nor breathe, nor stir,
But through the death of some of her...
JOHN MASEFIELD - FROM C.L.M.

Most near, most dear, most loved and most far,
Under the window where I often found her
Sitting huge as Asia, seismic with laughter,
Gin and chicken helpless in her Irish hand,
Irresistible as Rabelais, but most tender for
The lame dogs and hurt birds that surround her...
GEORGE BARKER - TO MY MOTHER

Oh hush thee, my dove,
Oh hush thee, my rowan,
Oh hush thee, my lapwing,
My little brown bird...
    Hebridean lullaby

Who ran to help me when I fell,
And would some pretty story tell,
Or kiss the place and make it well?
My Mother...
    Anne Taylor

How the days went
while you were blooming within me
I remember each upon each -
the swelling changed planes of my body
and how you first fluttered, then jumped
and I thought it was my heart.

How the days wound down
and the turning of winter
I recall with you growing heavy
against the wind. I thought
now her hands
are formed, and her hair
has started to curl
now her teeth are done
now she sneezes.
Then the seed opened
I bore you one morning just before spring
My head rang like a fiery piston
my legs were towers between which
A new world was passing.

AUDRE LORDE - NOW THAT I AM FOREVER WITH CHILD

So for the mother's sake the child was dear,
And dearer was the mother for the child...

SAMUEL TAYLOR COLERIDGE - FROM SONNET TO A FRIEND

When I was a child, I spake as a child,
I understood as a child, I thought as a child:
but when I became a man,
I put away childish things...

1 CORINTHIANS 13

Man may work from sun to sun,
but women's work is never done.

ANON.

Looking through the window, he saw her seated in the rocking-chair with the child, already in its nightdress, sitting on her knee. The fair head with its wild, fierce hair was drooping towards the fire-warmth, which reflected on the bright cheeks and clear skin of the child, who seemed to be musing almost like a grown-up person. The mother's face was dark and still, and he saw, with a pang, that she was away back in the life that had been. The child's hair gleamed like spun glass, her face was illuminated till it seemed like wax lit up from the inside. The wind boomed strongly. Mother and child sat motionless, silent, the child staring with vacant dark eyes into the fire, the mother looking into space . . .

D H LAWRENCE : FROM *THE RAINBOW*

To-day I am writing on the verandah with the three babies, more persistent than mosquitoes, raging round me, and already several of the thirty fingers have been in the ink-pot and the owners consoled when duty pointed to rebukes. But who can rebuke such penitent and drooping sun-bonnets? I can see nothing but sun-bonnets and pinafores and nimble black legs...

ELIZABETH VON ARNIM - FROM
ELIZABETH AND HER GERMAN GARDEN

People who say they sleep like babies usually don't have one.

MOYRA BREMNER

It's not easy being a mother. If it were easy, fathers would do it.

DOROTHY ON THE GOLDEN GIRLS

And she brought forth her firstborn son, and wrapped him in swaddling clothes, and laid him in a manger, because there was no room for them in the inn...

ST LUKE 2:7

She had seen their birth and the birth of her love
for them as miraculous, but it was just as
miraculous when they first smiled, first sat up,
first babbled a sound that resembled, of course,
mama. The tedious days were filled with
miracles. When a baby first looks at you; when it
gets excited at seeing a ray of light and like a dog
pawing a gleam, tries to catch it in his hand; or
when it laughs that deep, unselfconscious gurgle;
or when it cries and you pick it up and it clings
sobbing to you, saved from some terrible shadow
moving across the room, or a loud clang in the
street, or perhaps, already, a bad dream: then you
are – happy is not the precise word – filled.

MARILYN FRENCH - FROM *THE WOMEN'S ROOM*

One form of heroism – the most common, and yet the least remembered of all – namely, the heroism of the average mother. Ah! When I think of that broad fact, I gather hope again for poor humanity...

CHARLES KINGSLEY

The moment you have children yourself, you forgive your parents everything...

SUSAN HILL

Cedric stood with the big psalter open in his hands, singing with all his childish might, his face a little uplifted, happily; and as he sang, a long ray of sunshine crept in and slanting through a golden pane of a stained-glass window brightened the falling hair about his young head. His mother, as she looked at him across the church, felt a thrill pass through her heart, and a prayer rose in it too; a prayer that the pure, simple happiness of his childish soul might last, and that the strange, great fortune which had fallen to him might bring no wrong or evil with it...

FRANCIS HODGSON BURNETT - FROM *LITTLE LORD FAUNTLEROY*

Once upon a time in the depths of winter a queen sat sewing by her window, which was framed in black ebony, and watched the snowflakes as they fluttered like feathers from the sky to the earth below. And as she sewed and gazed at the snow, she pricked her finger with a needle and three drops of blood fell upon the snow. The red on the white snow looked very beautiful and made her think: 'If only I had a child white as snow and red as blood and dark as the ebony frame of this window.' Soon afterwards she gave birth to a little daughter who was indeed white as snow, red and blood and dark as ebony wood, and because of this she was called Little Snow-White ...

THE BROTHERS GRIMM -
FROM *SNOW-WHITE AND
THE SEVEN DWARFS*

With a feeling of suspense, she opened Oliver's door. He was sleeping quietly with his arms thrown above his head, fingers curled to the palms. On the pillow beside him, he had placed a little cobra made of green and yellow plasticine. It was curled in a spiral and reared up its flattened hood. Its eyes were the two halves of the aspirin she had given him to take with his Bengers. His forked tongue was one of her hairpins, which often scattered over his bed when she kissed him goodnight. The sight of the little plasticine snake quite tore from her heart the tendrils of anxiety which had grown there as she read Mrs Lippincote's *Home Nursing Encyclopaedia* . . .

ELIZABETH TAYLOR -
FROM *AT MRS LIPPINCOTE'S*

What can I say, but that it's not easy?
I cannot lift the stones out of your way,
And I can't cry your bitter tears for you.
I wonder if I could, what can I say?
But we're not one, we're worlds apart.
You and I,
Child of my body, bone of my bone,
Apple of my eye...

ROSALIE SORRELS - FROM APPLE OF MY EYE

Mama seemed to do only what my father
wanted, and yet we lived the way my
mother wanted us to live.

LILIAN HELLMAN

A mother is a person who seeing there are only four pieces of pie for five people, promptly anounces that she never did care for pie.

TENNEVA JORDAN

If you bungle raising your children, I don't think whatever else you do well matters very much.

JACQUELINE KENNEDY ONASSIS

Oh, to be half as wonderful as my child thought I was when he was small, and only half as stupid as my teenager now thinks I am.

REBECCA RICHARDS

My sole consolation when I went upstairs for the night was that Mamma would come in and kiss me after I was in bed. But this good night lasted for so short a time, she went down again so soon, that the moment in which I heard her climb the stairs, and then caught the sound of her garden dress of blue muslin, from which hung little tassels of plaited straw, rustling along the double-doored corridor, was for me a moment of the utmost pain; for it heralded the moment which was bound to follow it, when she would have left me and gone downstairs again...

MARCEL PROUST - FROM
REMEMBRANCE OF THINGS PAST

But see! The Virgin blest
Hath laid her Babe to rest...

JOHN MILTON - FROM ODE ON THE
MORNING OF CHRIST'S NATIVITY

Both nuns and mothers worship images,
But those the candles light are not as those
That animate a mother's reveries,
But keep a marble or a bronze repose.
And yet they too break hearts...

W. B. YEATS - AMONG SCHOOL CHILDREN

Happy he
With such a mother!
Faith in womankind
Beats with his blood...

ALFRED, LORD TENNYSON -
THE PRINCESS

The firelight was playing on her bent head, and as I looked at her I thought, our Kate's bonny. And at this point she looked at me and smiled, and as she did so my thought developed and said, She's more than bonny, she's beautiful is our Kate. She bent her head again and began to hum, then shortly she was singing...

'Speak! speak! speak to me, Thora
Speak from your heaven to me;
Child of my dreams, love of my life
Hope of my world to be!'

Child of my dreams, love of my life. Hope of my world to be... Her face, the firelight and her singing was too much. I choked and began to cry. She stopped in surprise, and putting her hand across the mat and stroking my head said, 'Aw! lass, don't don't. Come on. What is it? Don't.' Then she added in a conspiratorial way, 'Let's have a cup of tea and a bit of cake afore they come in, eh?'

On that day in the kitchen with the help of the firelight and her voice we became close, we became one. At rare moments in our lives we touched like this...

CATHERINE COOKSON - FROM *OUR KATE - AN AUTOBIOGRAPHY*

She is my first, great love. She was
a wonderful, rare woman - you do
not know; as strong, and steadfast,
and generous as the sun. She could
be swift as a white whip-lash, and
as kind and gentle as warm rain,
and steadfast as the irreducible
earth beneath us...

       D.H. LAWRENCE - ON HIS MOTHER

'I have no name:
I am but two days old.'
What shall I call thee?
'I happy am,
Joy is my name.'
Sweet joy befall thee!

Pretty joy!
Sweet joy but two days old,
Sweet joy I call thee:
Thou dost smile,
I sing the while,
Sweet joy befall thee!

       WILLIAM BLAKE - INFANT JOY

Then up rose Mrs Cratchit, Cratchit's wife, dressed out but poorly in a twice-turned gown, but brave in ribbons, which are cheap and make a goodly show for sixpence; and she laid the cloth, assisted by Belinda Cratchit, second of her daughters, also brave in ribbons; while Master Peter Cratchit plunged a fork into the saucepan of potatoes, and getting the corners of his monstrous shirt collar (Bob's private property, conferred upon his son and heir in honour of the day) into his mouth, rejoiced to find himself so gallantly attired, and yearned to show his linen in the fashionable Parks. And now two smaller Cratchits, boy and girl, came tearing in, screaming that outside the baker's they had smelt the goose, and known it for their own; and basking in luxurious thoughts of sage and onion, these young Cratchits danced about the table...

'What has ever got your precious father then?' said Mrs Cratchit. 'And your brother, Tiny Tim! And Martha warn't as late as this last Christmas Day, by half-an-hour?'

'Here's Martha, mother!' said a girl, appearing as she spoke.

'Here's Martha, mother!' cried the two young Cratchits. 'Hurrah! There's such a goose, Martha!'

'Why, bless your heart alive, my dear, how late you are!' said Mrs Cratchit, kissing her a dozen times, and taking off her shawl and bonnet for her with officious zeal...

CHARLES DICKENS - FROM *A CHRISTMAS CAROL*

...Hers the patience
Of one who made no claims, but simply loved
Because that was her nature, and loving so
Asked no more than to be repaid in kind.
If she was not a saint, I do not know
What saints are...

C. Day-Lewis - My Mother's Sister

Behold the Child among his new-born blisses,
A four year's Darling of a pigmy size!
See, where 'mid work of his own hand he lies,
Fretted by sallies of his Mother's kisses...

William Wordsworth -
from Intimations of Immortality

Then Phyllis said, 'Mother, didn't you ever walk on the railway lines when you were little?'

Mother was an honest and honorable Mother, so she had to say, 'Yes.'

'Well, then,' said Phyllis.

'But, darlings, you don't know how fond I am of you. What should I do if you got hurt?'

'Are you fonder of us than Granny was of you when you were little?' Phyllis asked. Bobbie made signs at her to stop, but Phyllis never did see signs, no matter how plain they might be.

Mother did not answer for a minute. She got up to put more water in the teapot.

'No one,' she said at last, 'ever loved anyone more than my mother loved me.'

Then she was quiet again, and Bobbie kicked Phyllis hard under the table, because Bobbie understood a little bit the thoughts that were making Mother so quiet - the thoughts of the time when Mother was a little girl and was all the world to her mother. It seems so easy and natural to run to Mother when one is in trouble. Bobbie understood a little how people do not leave off running to their mothers when they are in trouble even when they are grown-up, and she thought she knew a little what it must be to be sad, and have no mother to run to any more ...

E. NESBITT - FROM *THE RAILWAY CHILDREN*

Becoming a mother makes you the mother of all children. From now on each wounded, abandoned, frightened child is yours. You live in the suffering mothers of every race and creed and weep with them. You long to comfort all who are desolate.

CHARLOTTE GRAY

If help and salvation are to come, they can only come from the children, for the children are the makers of men.

MARIA MONTESSORI

'Glad to find you so merry, my girls,' said a cheery voice at the door, and actors and audience turned to welcome a tall, motherly lady, with a 'can-I-help-you' look about her which was truly delightful. She was not elegantly dressed, but a noble-looking woman, and the girls thought the grey cloak and unfashionable bonnet covered the most splendid mother in the world...

LOUISA MAY ALCOTT - FROM *LITTLE WOMEN*

'Dear Mother,' she began again. 'There are moments in which you appear tender, like a snapshot melting, tinged with beauty and grace, imparting the same vague sorrow as when one sees an old man or a young child at a farmhouse, staring, the child waving but not sure if the wave is seen and losing heart in the middle of it. You would come down to the yard, your hands smeared with meal, a few eggs in a can, but never enough; they would be dunged and covered in meal and the one above all others I remember is the shell-less egg, soft as any placenta, its bruisedness a resemblance of us. If only we could have imagined ourselves into each other's depths. If only!'

EDNA O'BRIEN - FROM *TIME AND TIDE*

Making the decision to have a child - it's momentous. It is to decide forever to have your heart go walking around outside your body.

ELIZABETH STONE

A mother is she who can take the place of all others but whose place no one else can take.

CARDINAL MERMILLOD

As one whom his mother comforted, so will I comfort you...

SONG OF SOLOMON, 66:13

I love Felix to distraction. I am sure the love would be exactly the same temperature if I had been blessed with a daughter instead, but doubt that I would be enslaved in quite the same way. It is the stormiest love affair of my life...

In the midst of intense and complicated negotiations with him, a mist lifts from my eyes, and I see how little he is. He really is a baby, for God's sake. I am being ruled by someone with dimpled knuckles.

A baby, but a shockingly self-aware one, constantly revolving the advantages that might or might not accrue to the state of babydom. He is always checking his little cousin, eighteen months younger than himself, for signs of usurpation. He cannot decide whether to compete with her in the baby stakes, or flaunt his superior age and attainments.

'Elsa can't talk, can she?'

'Not as well as you,' says Elsa's mother tactfully, 'but she knows lots of words. She can say "dog", and "cat", and -'

'Can she,' interrupts Felix sternly, 'say "microwave"?'...

KATE SAUNDERS - FROM *THIS CRYING THING*

'In my next incarnation,' my mother said once, 'I'm going to be an archaeologist and go round digging things up.' We were sitting on the bed that had once been my brother's, then mine, then my sister's; we were sorting out things from one of the trunks, deciding what could now be given away or thrown out. My mother believes that what you save from the past is mostly a matter of choice... This statement of hers startled me. It was the first time I'd ever heard my mother say that she might have wanted to be something other than she was. I must have been thirty-five at the time, but it was still shocking and slightly offensive to me to learn that my mother might not have been totally contented fulfilling the role in which fate had cast her: that of being my mother. What thumb-suckers we all are, I thought, when it came to mothers.

Shortly after this I became a mother myself, and this moment altered for me...

MARGARET ATWOOD - FROM *SIGNIFICANT MOMENTS IN THE LIFE OF MY MOTHER*

God knows how infantine the memory may have been, that was awakened within me by the sound of my mother's voice in the old parlour, when I set foot in the hall. She was singing in a low tone. I think I must have lain in her arms, and heard her singing so to me when I was but a baby. The strain was new to me, and yet it was so old that it filled my heart brim-full; like a friend come back from a long absence.

I believed, from the solitary and thoughtful way in which my mother murmured her song, that she was alone. And I went softly into the room...

CHARLES DICKENS - FROM
DAVID COPPERFIELD

A child's kiss set on thy singing lips shall make thee glad:
A poor child served by thee shall make thee rich;
A sick child helped by thee shall make thee strong;
Thou shalt be served thyself by every sense of service
   which thou renderest.

ELIZABETH BARRETT BROWNING

A mother is not a person to lean on, but a person
to make leaning unnecessary.

DOROTHY CANFIELD FISHER

Mothers have as powerful an influence
  over the welfare of future
  generations as all other
  earthly causes combined.

JOHN S.C. ABBOTT

Motherly love is not much use if it expresses itself only as a warm gush of emotion, delicately tinged with pink. It must also be strong, guiding and unselfish. The sweetly-sung lullaby, the cool hand on the fevered brow, the Mother's Day smiles and flowers are only a small part of the picture. True mothers have to be made of steel to withstand the difficulties that are sure to beset their children.

RACHEL BILLINGTON - FROM *THE GREAT UMBILICAL*

God could not be everywhere and so he made mothers.

JEWISH PROVERB

The best way to keep children home is to make the home atmosphere pleasant - and let the air out of the tires.

DOROTHY PARKER

Motherhood is neither a duty nor a privilege, but simply the way that humanity can satisfy the desire for physical immortality and triumph over the fear of death.

REBECCA WEST

But, as a baby, this baby was all that could be desired. This fact no one attempted to deny. 'Is he not delightful?' she would say to her father, looking up into his face from her knees, her lustrous eyes overflowing with soft tears, her young face encircled by her close widow's cap and her hands on each side of the cradle in which her treasure was sleeping.

The grandfather would gladly agree that the treasure was delightful, and the uncle archdeacon himself would agree, and Mrs Grantly, Eleanor's sister, would re-echo the word with true sisterly energy; and Mary Bold - but Mary Bold was a second worshipper at the same shrine.

The baby was really delightful; he took his food with a will, stuck out his toes merrily whenever his legs were uncovered, and did not have fits. These are supposed to be the strongest points of baby perfection, and in all these our baby excelled.

And thus the widow's deep grief was softened, and a sweet balm was poured into the wound which she had thought nothing but death could heal...

ANTHONY TROLLOPE - FROM BARCHESTER TOWERS

It is the nightly custom of every good mother after her children are asleep to rummage in their minds and put things straight for the next morning, repacking into their proper places the many articles that have wandered during the day...

When you awake in the morning the naughtiness and evil passions with which you went to bed have been folded up very small and placed at the bottom of your mind; and on top, beautifully aired, are spread out your prettier thoughts, ready for you to put on.

J.M. Barrie - from *Peter Pan*

There is in all this world
no fount of deep, strong,
deathless love,
save that within
a mother's heart.

Felicia Hemans

It was pleasant to see that large family in the hush and reverence of such teaching, the mother's gentle power preventing the outbreaks of recklessness to which even at such times the wild young spirits are liable. Margaret and Miss Winter especially rejoiced in it on this occasion, the first since the birth of the baby, that she had been able to preside. Under her, though seemingly without her taking any trouble, there was none of the smothered laughter at the little ones' mistakes, the fidgeting of the boys, of Harry's audacious impertinence to Miss Winter; and no less glad was Harry to have his mother there, and be guarded from himself…

CHARLOTTE M. YONGE - FROM *THE DAISY CHAIN*

I know how to do anything – I'm a mom.
SROSEANNE BARR ARNOLD

You see much more of your children once they
leave home.
LUCILLE BALL

O hush thee, my babie, thy sire was a knight,
Thy mother a lady, both lovely and bright…
SIR WALTER SCOTT - LULLABY OF AN INFANT CHIEF

She put her in my arms and I sat there looking at her, and her great wide blue eyes looked at me with seeming recognition, and what I felt it is pointless trying to describe. Love, I suppose one might call it, and the first of my life...

MARGARET DRABBLE - FROM *THE MILLSTONE*

If the hours are long enough and the pay short enough, someone will say it's women's work.

ANON.

James James
Morrison Morrison
Weatherby George Dupree
Took great
Care of his Mother
Though he was only
    three...

A. A. MILNE - FROM
DISOBEDIENCE

There seemed to be something huge and important to say;
But somehow, then, we could never think of the words.
Anyway, they would keep, so it did not matter,
And there would be time and time enough to remember;
So we laughed as the years flew over our heads like birds.

And then, one day, we remembered them; ran all the way
Breathless came running, and beat and called at your door:
At the door of the house whose silence and emptiness mocked us,
For you had slipped out the back way, quite quietly, leaving
'I love you and thank you,' uneeded, unsaid, ever more,

MARGARET WILLY

When thou hast taken thy repast,
Repose, my babe, on me:
So may thy mother and thy nurse
Thy cradle also be.
Sing lullaby, my little boy,
Sing lullaby, my only joy!
ANON.

If evolution really works, how come mothers
only have two hands?
MILTON BERLE

Any mother could perform the jobs of several
air traffic controllers with ease.
LISA ALTHER

The only time a woman really succeeds in
changing a man is when he's a baby.
NATALIE WOOD

My mother loved children – she would have
given anything if I had been one.
GROUCHO MARX

I don't care how many babies are born a minute in the world. This boy was mine and the only one that mattered. A divine miracle. The ceaseless miracle, of life and birth and death... My baby, Paris. What Helen wouldn't willingly leave a thousand Menelauses for this miracle boy? I was in love and none of the rest mattered...

SOPHIE PARKIN - FROM *A BOY IN THE FAMILY*

From this day you must be a stranger
to one of your parents. Your mother
will never see you again if you do *not*
marry Mr Collins, and I will never see
you again if you *do*.

JANE AUSTEN - FROM *PRIDE AND PREJUDICE*

Golden slumbers kiss your eyes,
Smiles awake you when you rise,
Sleep, pretty darling, do not cry,
And I will sing a lullaby…

TRADITIONAL

43

I will go back to the great sweet mother
Mother and lover of men, the sea...

A. C. SWINBURNE - FROM THE TRIUMPH OF TIME

Certainly there she was, in the very centre of
that great Cathedral space which was
childhood; there she was from the very first.
My first memory is of her lap; the scratch of
some beads on her dress comes back to me as
I pressed my cheek against it. Then I see her
in her white dressing gown on the balcony;
and the passion flower with the purple star on
its petals. Her voice is still faintly in my ears –
decided, quick; and in particular the little
drops with which her laugh ended – three
diminishing ahs... 'Ah-ah-ah...' I sometimes
end a laugh that way myself...

VIRGINIA WOOLF - ON HER MOTHER

My dear Child,

I am extremely concerned to hear you complain of ill health at a time of life when you ought to be in the flower of your strength. I hope I need not recommend to you the care of it. The tenderness you have for your children is sufficient to enforce you to the preservation of a life so necessary to their well-being. I do not doubt your prudence in their education; neither can I say anything particular relating to it at this distance, different tempers requiring different management. In general, never attempt to govern them (as most people do) by deceit. If they find themselves cheated (even in trifles) it will so far lessen the authority of their instructor as to make them neglect all further admonitions. And (if possible) breed them free from prejudices; those contracted in the nursery often influence the whole life after, of which I have seen many melancholy examples...

LADY MARY WORTLEY MONTAGU - FROM A LETTER TO HER DAUGHTER, JANUARY 1750

Sing lullaby, as women do,
Wherewith they bring their babes to rest,
And lullaby can I sing too
As womanly as can the best.
With lullaby they still the child,
And if I be not much beguiled,
Full many wanton babes have I
Which must be stilled with lullaby…

GEORGE GASCOIGNE - FROM GASCOIGNE'S
LULLABY

All women become like their
mothers. That is their tragedy. No
man does. That's his.

OSCAR WILDE - *THE IMPORTANCE OF
BEING EARNEST*

In the man whose childhood had
known caresses and kindness, there
is always a fibre of memory that can
be touched to gentle issues.

GEORGE ELIOT

We can only learn to love by loving.

IRIS MURDOCH

Time is the only comforter for the
loss of a mother…

JANE WELSH CARLYLE

Mother, O mother, my heart calls for you!
Over my heart, in the days that are flown,
No love like mother love ever has shone.
No other worship abides and endures –
Faithful, unselfish, and patient like yours:
None like a mother can charm away pain
From the sick soul and the world-weary brain.
Over my slumbers your loving watch keep;
Rock me to sleep, mother – rock me to sleep!

ELIZABETH AKERS ALLEN